Countries of the World

Haiti

by Suzanne Paul Dell'Oro

Consultant:
John Kozyn
Consultant
Embassy of Haiti

Bridgestone Books
an imprint of Capstone Press
Mankato, Minnesota

Bridgestone Books are published by Capstone Press
151 Good Counsel Drive, P.O. Box 669, Mankato, Minnesota 56002
http://www.capstone-press.com

Library of Congress Cataloging-in-Publication Data
Dell'Oro, Suzanne Paul.
   Haiti/by Suzanne Paul Dell'Oro.
   p. cm.—(Countries of the world)
   Includes bibliographical references and index.
   ISBN 0-7368-0942-2
   1. Haiti—Juvenile literature. [1. Haiti.] I. Title. II. Countries of the world (Mankato, Minn.)
F1915.2 .D45 2002
972.94—dc21   00-012580

Summary: Discusses the landscape, culture, food, animals, sports, and holidays of Haiti.

Editorial Credits

Erika Mikkelson, editor; Karen Risch, product planning editor; Linda Clavel, designer and
   illustrator; Jeff Anderson, photo researcher

Photo Credits

DDB Stock Photo/Alyx Kellington, 6, 20; Kathleen Marie Rohr, 8, 18
Jason Lauré, 14
Kay Shaw, cover, 10, 12
One Mile Up, Inc., 5 (top)
Visuals Unlimited/Robert C. Simpson, 16

1 2 3 4 5 6 07 06 05 04 03 02

Table of Contents

Fast Facts

Name: Republic of Haiti
Capital: Port-au-Prince
Population: Almost 6.9 million
Languages: French, Creole
Religion: Mostly Roman Catholic

Size: 10,714 square miles
(27,749 square kilometers)
Haiti is about the same size as the U.S. state of Maryland.
Crops: Coffee, mangoes, sugarcane, rice, corn, sorghum

Maps

Atlantic Ocean

Ile de la Tortue

Haiti

Northern Chain

Noires Mountains

Artibonite River

Gulf of Gonâve

Ile de la Gonâve

Grande Cayemite

Lake Saumâtre

Port-au-Prince

La Selle Mount

Ile à Vache

DOMINICAN REPUBLIC

Caribbean Sea

HAITI

Flag

Haiti's flag has two horizontal stripes. The blue stripe is above the red stripe. Haiti's coat of arms lies in a white rectangle in the center of the flag. A palm tree on the coat of arms stands for freedom. A stocking cap on top of the palm tree stands for liberty. Flags and two cannons surround the tree. A sign below the tree says "L'Union Fait la Force." This French motto means "Union Makes Strength."

Currency

The unit of currency in Haiti is the gourde. One hundred centimes equal one gourde.

In the early 2000s, 23 gourdes equaled about 1 U.S. dollar. Fifteen gourdes equaled about 1 Canadian dollar.

The Land

Haiti is part of an island called Hispaniola in the Caribbean Sea. The Dominican Republic borders Haiti on the east. Haiti is shaped like a bird's head with an open beak. The Gulf of Gonâve lies inside the beak. Haiti's capital, Port-au-Prince, is located where the two parts of the beak meet.

Four small islands lie off Haiti's coast. These Haitian islands are Ile de la Gonâve, Ile de la Tortue, Grande Cayemite, and Ile à Vache.

Haiti's mainland is mostly mountains and hilly coastline. Haiti received its name from a Taino Indian word that means "has lots of mountains." The three largest mountain ranges are the Northern Chain, La Selle Mount, and the Noires Mountains.

The Artibonite River is Haiti's longest river. Haitians travel and ship goods on this river. The largest lake in Haiti is Lake Saumâtre. This lake is saltwater.

Mountains cover most of Haiti.

Life at Home

Two-thirds of Haitians live in the countryside. They grow food for their families. Farmers may trade or sell their food for other items they need.

Haitians may live in a one-room house called a caille (ka-EE) or lakay (la-KYE). These homes are made from concrete blocks. Cailles protect people from heat and rain.

Some people move from the countryside to the cities to find jobs. People who find jobs often are paid very little. They may rent one or two rooms for their entire family.

Haitians have strong family ties. People often live with or near relatives. They often eat meals together. Families spend time in the evening playing games and telling stories. They sometimes go on walks to visit relatives and friends. Families and their relatives often gather to celebrate holidays.

Some houses in Haiti are painted bright colors.

Going to School

Education is important to Haitians. They believe well-educated people can find good jobs. But many Haitian children cannot attend school. Some children must help their families by farming or by selling goods. Fewer than half of all Haitians know how to read and write.

Primary school is first grade through sixth grade. Classes are taught in the Creole language. Students also learn French. Half of the schools in Haiti are public schools supported by the government. The other half are run by churches.

In high school, classes are taught in French. Students also learn English. Wealthy families sometimes send their children to France or to the United States for high school. Some students choose to attend a university in France or in the United States after high school.

Students in Haiti learn to speak French.

Haitian Food

Most Haitians grow their own food. They often raise beans, rice, corn, and yams. Haitians also eat oranges, grapefruit, avocados, and mangoes.

Many Haitians might eat only one small meal per day. This midday meal often is porridge made from corn, rice, or sorghum. Sorghum is a sweet syrup made from grass.

Haitians may eat small snacks throughout the day. People drink coffee with manioc sour bread. Manioc is a thick paste pounded from the root of the manioc plant. Haitians also chew on sugarcane as a snack.

Haitians enjoy the spicy and rich taste of Creole cooking. Kalalou (kah-lah-LOO) is a typical Creole dish. It is a mixture of pork, crabmeat, spinach, okra, chili peppers, and onions. Another Creole food is pain patate (paihn pah-TAT). This pudding is made with potatoes, figs, bananas, and sugar.

Beans and rice are important foods in Haiti.

Clothes

Haitians wear loose, lightweight clothing because the weather is hot in Haiti. People make their clothes from colorful cotton or linen. Women usually wear dresses. Men stay cool in short-sleeved shirts and cotton pants.

Traditional Creole dancers dress in old French style. Men wear baggy pants and stocking caps. Women wear big skirts and wrap scarves around their heads. Dancers perform barefoot.

During Vodou (VOO-doo) ceremonies, Haitians may follow African traditions. They sometimes dress in brightly colored clothing.

Carnival is a time for special clothes. Carnival is a celebration six weeks before Easter. People make their own costumes to wear in parades. They sew suits of bright or shiny pieces of cloth. They wear feathers, make-up, and masks.

Haitians wear lightweight clothing to keep cool.

Animals

Many animals thrive in Haiti's warm, rainy areas. Haiti's lakes, rivers, and forests are home to many animals. They include alligators, chameleons, rhino-horned iguanas, and lizards.

Water birds such as flamingos and egrets live in Haiti. More than 200 other kinds of birds eat Haiti's many insects. Spiders, centipedes, and scorpions crawl throughout Haiti.

More than 270 kinds of fish swim in Haiti's waters. Haitians fish for tuna, anchovies, and other fish. Barracuda and colorful tropical fish also live off Haiti's coast.

Many people have cut down forests where Haiti's animals live. Some people try to protect these animals by placing them in reserves and parks. The Macaya Biosphere Reserve is a native pine forest. The Parc La Visite is another reserve. These parks are home to animals such as butterflies, bats, crocodiles, and parrots.

Flamingos are one of Haiti's many kinds of birds.

Sports and Recreation

Sports that require few pieces of equipment are popular in Haiti. Many children in Haiti play soccer. If nobody has a ball, players make one from whatever they can find.

Haitians also enjoy dancing. People often gather to listen to music and to dance. Haitians call these gatherings bamboches (bam-BOSHS).

Haitians play games in their free time. Children might play with osselets. These dice are made of goat knuckles. Some Haitians might play dominoes. Dominoes are flat tiles with dots at each end. Players must match the number of dots as they lay their dominoes. Children also play tag and hopscotch.

Haitians enjoy playing soccer.

Holidays and Celebrations

Many Haitians practice Vodou. People who practice Vodou believe in the spirits of their ancestors. Many celebrations honor Vodou spirits.

November 2 is the Day of the Dead. On this day, Haitians remember their friends and relatives who have died. They visit graveyards, pray, and take food to the dead. Some people set a place at the table for a friend or relative who has died.

Haitians celebrate other holidays. On Christmas, Haitians go to church at midnight. They eat a special supper. Some families open gifts. Carnival occurs before Easter. Haitians throw parties and have parades during this festival.

On January 1, Haitians celebrate Independence Day. Haiti became independent from France on this day in 1804. Today, people hold parades to celebrate. Families prepare a special dinner. Children sometimes receive presents from family members.

Some Haitians wear costumes during Carnival.

Hands On: Play Osselets

Haitian children often play osselets. You can make your own osselets and play the game.

What You Need

5 dice

Masking tape

Marker

At least 2 players

What You Do

1. Wrap the five dice in masking tape. Mark each die with a 2, +, I, and S. One symbol goes on a side. The remaining two sides should be blank.
2. Toss all five dice on the ground.
3. Then throw any die into the air. At the same time, grab a die that shows a 2. If none of the dice shows a 2, turn one to 2 before grabbing it.
4. In the same hand, catch the first die before it falls to the ground.
5. Now you have two dice. Without putting them down, throw one of them into the air. Turn a third die to 2, then grab it. Catch the die that you threw in the air. Now you have three dice. Continue until you have all five dice in your hand.
6. If you miss, another player takes a turn. Each time you miss, you begin your next turn with only one die.

Learn to Speak Creole

Hello	Bonjou	(bohn-ZHOU)
Please	Tanpri souple	(TAWN-pree SOOP-lay)
Thank You	Mési	(MEH-si)
Father	Papa	(pah-PAH)
Mother	Manman	(mawn-MAWN)
Yes	Wi	(WEE)
No	Non	(NOHN)

Words to Know

Carnival (CAR-nuh-vuhl)—a festival celebrated the weeks before Easter

coat of arms (KOHT UHV ARMZ)—a shield or a picture of a shield that has a design on it; the design usually is the symbol for a family, city, state, or country.

Creole (KREE-ohl)—a language spoken in Haiti; Creole is taken from the French language; Creole also means food prepared with a spicy sauce of tomatoes and peppers.

domino (DOM-uh-noh)—a small rectangular tile that is divided into two halves that are blank or contain dots

sorghum (SORE-guhm)—a sweet syrup made from grass

tradition (truh-DISH-uhn)—a custom, idea, or belief handed down from one generation to the next

Read More

Schemenauer, Elma. *Haiti.* Faces and Places. Chanhassen, Minn.: Child's World, 2001.

Will, Emily Wade. *Haiti.* Modern Nations of the World. San Diego: Lucent Books, 2001.

Useful Addresses and Internet Sites

Consulate General of Haiti
1801 McGill Avenue, Suite 1335
Montreal, QC   H3A 2N4
Canada

Embassy of the Republic of Haiti
2311 Massachusetts Avenue NW
Washington, DC 20008

CIA World Factbook—Haiti
http://www.odci.gov/cia/publications/factbook/geos/ha.html
The Embassy of the Republic of Haiti, Washington, D.C.
http://www.haiti.org/

Index